Medieval Knights

Adam Woog

KIDHAVEN PRESS™

THOMSON
™
GALE

San Diego • Detroit • New York • San Francisco • Cleveland
New Haven, Conn. • Waterville, Maine • London • Munich

Special thanks to Stu Witmer for research help.
Hey, Stu—you've got mail!

© 2003 by KidHaven Press. KidHaven Press is an imprint of The Gale Group, Inc., a division of Thomson Learning, Inc.

KidHaven™ and Thomson Learning™ are trademarks used herein under license.

For more information, contact
KidHaven Press
27500 Drake Rd.
Farmington Hills, MI 48331-3535
Or you can visit our Internet site at http://www.gale.com

LIBRARY OF CONGRESS CATALOGING-IN-PUBLICATION DATA

Woog, Adam, 1953–
   Medieval knights / By Adam Woog.
   p. cm. — (Daily life)
Summary: Describes the life of a medieval knight, including home and family life, training, weapons, armor, horses, battles, and codes of ethics and honor. Includes bibliographical references.
   ISBN 0-7377-0992-8 (alk. paper)
   1. Knights and knighthood—Juvenile literature. [1. Knights and knighthood.
   2. Middle Ages. 3. Civilization, Medieval.] I. Title. II. Series.
   CR4513 .W66 2003
   940.1'088'355—dc21
                                                                    2002015473

Printed in China

Contents

CHAPTER ONE

What Was a Knight?

T he medieval era, which lasted from about the sixth to the fifteenth century in Europe, was a violent, uncertain, and exciting time. Stories about knights, the professional warriors of this era, can still thrill us even after hundreds of years.

Most medieval soldiers were ordinary men. They fought on foot with spears, arrows, or crossbows and wore only a little armor. Knights were different. They fought on horses, used swords and other powerful weapons, and wore full armor. Knights were the most important soldiers of their time.

A knight was a powerful killing machine, far deadlier than a regular soldier. Being on horseback gave him an advantage in height and speed. He could slash viciously down at foot soldiers and ride quickly in or out of battle. A fifteenth-century writer noted that "a brave man, mounted on a good horse, may do more in an hour of fighting than ten or mayhap [perhaps] a hundred could afoot."[1]

A Wild Patchwork

Knights began to appear in about the year 500, as the aristocrats who were in power across Europe organized their own armies. These armies were needed because there were no strong central governments. Instead, Europe was a wild patchwork of small governments, some no bigger than a modern county or small town.

Dressed in armor, a knight rides his spirited horse.

Some kings and queens controlled large regions, such as France or England. Even these rulers, however, had to struggle to organize the many independent governments within their borders that were controlled by lesser leaders, called lords.

Within their regions, these lords were the absolute authority. They administered justice, minted their own money, gathered taxes, and managed crop production. They could even decide who their subjects could and could not marry.

All of these lords needed to maintain strong armies because they were constantly battling each other over border disputes and other matters. Knights began as hired soldiers in these armies.

By the twelfth century, knights had greatly risen in status. They became part of the nobility itself. All kings and lesser lords were knights (although not all knights were lords).

This change in social standing happened partly because warfare was such an important part of life. Battle was seen as glorious and noble, and knights were the top soldiers.

Knights were often happiest when they were fighting and bored if they were not. An eleventh-century writer noted that knights on their way to fight "sang warlike songs so joyously that they seemed to look upon the approaching battle as if it were a sport."[2]

A Part of Feudalism

A complex social system called **feudalism** defined the ties between kings, lords, and lesser knights. It was based on how land and money were distributed.

Saint George, a legendary knight, slays the dragon. Knights were known for their heroic feats.

The economy of medieval Europe was based on farming. Money was scarce, so land equaled wealth. Nobles had lots of land, and they needed the help of knights. Knights, meanwhile, needed income because it was expensive to buy and maintain horses, armor, and

A family farms a knight's fief. Income from his fief helped the knight pay for armor, horses, and weapons.

weapons. So a system arose that passed land from the most powerful aristocrats down to lesser knights.

Kings gave out land to lesser lords, such as dukes or earls. These gifts were then divided further, with smaller parcels going to knights in the lords' employ.

These gifts of property were called **fiefs**. The land still belonged to the lord who gave it, but a knight with a fief was allowed to keep whatever was produced from it.

Sometimes a fief was not land. It could be something else that made money, such as a mill or a license to collect taxes in a certain area. However, the vast majority of fiefs were land. The practice of giving fiefs was used all over the continent. By the end of the twelfth century most of the land in western and central Europe was in the hands of knights.

A Solemn Promise

In return for receiving a fief from a lord, a knight promised to give him a part of what the land produced. He also made a solemn promise of loyalty. This was called an **oath of fealty**.

The knight swore in a special ceremony that he would be his lord's man forever. He promised to fight for the

Sworn to protect his lord (center, wearing crown), a knight (left) strikes down an attacker.

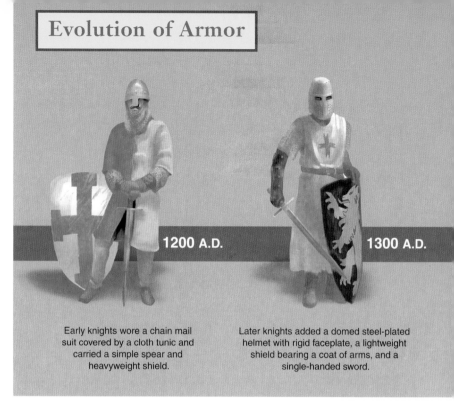

Evolution of Armor

1200 A.D.

1300 A.D.

Early knights wore a chain mail suit covered by a cloth tunic and carried a simple spear and heavyweight shield.

Later knights added a domed steel-plated helmet with rigid faceplate, a lightweight shield bearing a coat of arms, and a single-handed sword.

lord—to the death, if necessary—and to supply him with other knights and soldiers when needed. Typically, a knight promised to fight for his lord forty days out of each year.

For example, in the twelfth century King Henry I of England every year paid five hundred pounds—a vast fortune—to Count Robert II of Flanders. In return, Robert promised that the knights under him, over a thousand men, stood ready to defend Henry against his bitter enemy, Philip I of France.

Knights also promised to feed and shelter their lords when kings traveled through their fiefs. This duty could be expensive. William the Conqueror, the Norman who invaded England in 1066, stopped one Christmas at the estate of one of his lords. In just a few days of feasting William and his company of men ate 6,000 chickens,

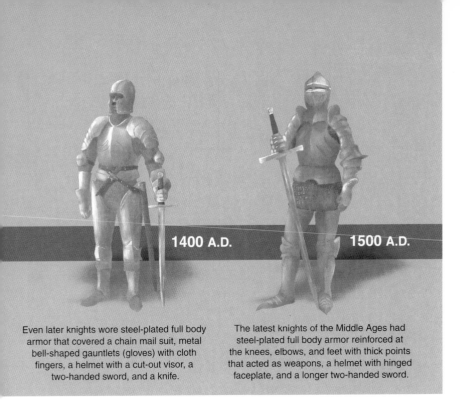

Even later knights wore steel-plated full body armor that covered a chain mail suit, metal bell-shaped gauntlets (gloves) with cloth fingers, a helmet with a cut-out visor, a two-handed sword, and a knife.

The latest knights of the Middle Ages had steel-plated full body armor reinforced at the knees, elbows, and feet with thick points that acted as weapons, a helmet with hinged faceplate, and a longer two-handed sword.

1,000 rabbits, 90 boars, 50 peacocks, 200 geese, 10,000 eels, thousands of eggs and loaves of bread, and hundreds of casks of wine and cider.

The Next Sons

The sons of knights were allowed to become knights themselves. However, according to medieval custom, only the first son inherited a father's main possessions. Therefore, when a knight died, only his firstborn son could become a knight and also inherit the family's fief.

All of a knight's other sons had to find their own ways in the world. Many second, third, or fourth sons naturally also chose knighthood as a path to success and survival. These knights without fiefs typically attached themselves to lords who could pay them salaries. Many of these landless knights lived fairly humble lives in the castles of their lords.

Sometimes, however, sons who did not inherit wealth found it on their own. William Marshal, who lived in the twelfth century, was the fourth son of a nobleman who had served King Henry I of England. Since he could not inherit his father's land, William trained to be a knight and became a distinguished aide to several English kings.

In return for his excellent service, William was allowed to marry a wealthy woman and receive many estates in England, Wales, and Ireland. By the time of his death, William Marshal was one of the richest and most titled men in England.

William Marshal, like all knights, needed enough money, the right family, and social connections. Becoming a knight also required years of training.

CHAPTER TWO

Training for Knighthood

A boy's dreams of becoming a knight—and his training for knighthood—began when he was only a few years old. First, his mother and nurses taught him the basics of proper noble behavior, such as good manners, religious faith, and service to others.

Sometimes at this point he also began learning foreign languages, reading, and writing. Although these skills were not required for knighthood, a gentleman was expected to be well educated.

When he was four or five, the boy received a precious gift—a pony. He learned how to handle horses by riding across his father's land, and he learned to care for horses by feeding and brushing his animal. His teachers in this were usually the stablemen who worked for his father.

Pages

When he was about seven, the boy became a **page**. This was an apprentice, or junior assistant, to a knight. His new master was not his father, but usually a relative or family friend.

A young knight in training. Boys with dreams of knighthood had to master many skills.

A page lived in his master's home. Sometimes this was close to his own family home, but often a page had to travel far to start his new life. For example, William Marshal was sent from his home in England to France. In those days, this was a difficult journey of days or even weeks by horse and small boat. Like all travelers, William faced such obstacles as poor roads, bad weather, robbers, and pirates.

In France, William served as a page to his cousin, a knight who was in service to the duke of Normandy. William had many jobs, including such household errands as sweeping out rooms and carrying water from the well. He also had to help care for his master's weapons and armor. It was hard, exhausting work.

A page got no salary for all this labor, but he did get useful training. One of the most important skills he learned was to hunt wild animals. He did this with his first serious weapon, a bow and arrow. Hunting was a good way to get food, but it was also excellent training for battle. While hunting a fast-moving target in deep woods, a page had to think quickly and wisely.

Knights had to be expert horsemen, both in hunting and in battle.

Squires

Between the ages of fourteen and sixteen a page became a **squire**. He was still an apprentice to a knight, but now he had more responsibilities.

For instance, he had to serve his master's meals, including carving his meat. He had to care for his master's weapons and armor, look after his horse, and help him dress and undress. At night a squire slept just outside his master's bedroom, or even across his doorstep.

When his master needed to get into armor for battle, the process of helping him prepare could take hours. When the knight rode off to battle, his squire took care of the extra horses and supplies, carried the spare weapons, and otherwise helped out.

Such responsibilities were considered essential to proper training. A thirteenth-century knight wrote that "the son of a knight should learn how to serve, before he becomes a lord, or he would not understand how noble is the authority of a knight."[3]

Life was not all responsibilities, however. Squires also had many privileges. They were allowed to own their own swords, helmets, and shields. Also, a squire continued to receive training from his master and the household staff.

He learned advanced horsemanship and hunting, and how to use weapons such as swords and **lances**. The most common type of sword was a wide, double-edged **broadsword**. Broadswords could be used with one hand, since they were only about two and a half feet long and about three pounds.

Knights joust in a tournament. Squires had to master the art of fighting with lances.

Lances were wooden-tipped spears about twelve feet long. Knights charging on horseback tried to spear each other with them.

Such hands-on training with these could be rough. One medieval writer noted, "A youth must have seen his blood flow and felt his teeth crack under the blow of his adversary and have been thrown to the ground twenty times [to] be able to face real war with the hope of victory."[4]

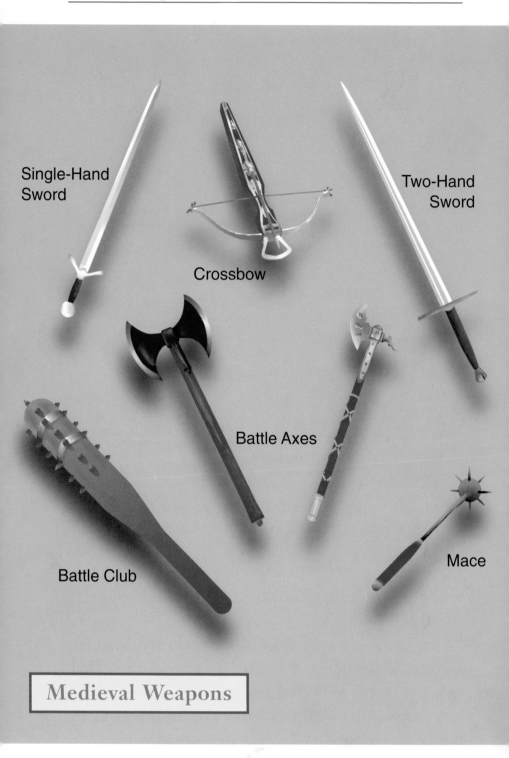

Single-Hand
Sword

Two-Hand
Sword

Crossbow

Battle Axes

Battle Club

Mace

Medieval Weapons

Becoming a Knight

When he was in his teens or early twenties, a squire could finally become a knight. Not every squire would become one, however. First, the candidate had to pass tests of strength, courage, character, and skill with weapons. For example, he might be sent into the woods alone and told he could not return until he had killed a certain number of animals. Also, he had to prove he had enough income to maintain expensive horses, servants, and armor.

Many failed these tests, especially when it came to having enough money. Some squires remained squires, in service to other knights, all their lives.

Other squires did not become knights until much later in life. For instance, Bertrand de Guesclin, one of the most famous knights of the fourteenth century, did not come from a wealthy family. He served as a regular soldier until he was thirty-four, when he finally earned enough money to become a knight.

Usually, squires became knights in a special ritual called a **dubbing ceremony**. By the twelfth century, this ceremony had become quite elaborate. Since knighthood was closely connected to Christianity, the ritual usually took place on a major religious holiday, such as Easter. Often many young men became knights on the same day.

"I Dub Thee . . ."

On the day before the dubbing ceremony, a knight-to-be went to church, laid his sword on the altar to be blessed, and spent the night in prayer. The next day he took a special bath to symbolically wash away his sins. Then he donned special clothing, with an experienced knight solemnly buckling on his sword and spurs for him.

He and the others then knelt, one after another, before a veteran knight. This knight struck each knight-to-be on the shoulder or head. Sometimes the knight struck with his hand, sometimes with the flat of a sword. Sometimes the blow was light, but sometimes it knocked the kneeling man over. In any case, the blow symbolized, among other things, the last time the new knight could ever be struck without taking revenge.

When each young man rose to his feet, he was formally a knight. The rest of the day was spent celebrating the great event with feasts, drinking bouts, and contests of skill.

The knights also got gifts from their sponsors in honor of their new status—perhaps a suit of armor, a decorated cloak, or, in the case of fifteen-year-old Geoffrey of Anjours, "a Spanish horse of wondrous beauty . . . swifter than the flight of birds."[5]

Such gifts were essential for fighting battles. And armed conflict was what a knight lived for.

CHAPTER THREE

In Battle

Knights liked battle for many reasons. It tested their courage and fighting skills. It was also a path to glory, since brave knights were remembered as great heroes.

Perhaps most important of all, battle was a way for knights to add to the regular incomes they received from fiefs. One common way to do this was to capture enemy knights and hold them for ransom. These noble prisoners could be worth hundreds of thousands of dollars in today's money.

Knights also enriched themselves by looting enemy castles and villages, taking everything of value. One fifteenth-century observer wrote that the enthusiastic winners of a battle "carried off with them whatever they could come upon or discover, whether garments or money, herds of cattle or single animals."[6]

Raids and Sieges

Knights did not often fight large, organized battles on open fields. When big conflicts did occur, they became famous. An example is the Battle of Agincourt in 1415—the final battle in the Hundred Years' War between England and France.

Knights engage in battle. Battle brought glory and riches to knights.

Such large-scale battles were so unusual that even the most active knights fought in only a handful. In his sixty years as a celebrated soldier, for instance, Bertrand de Guesclin fought in only about six large battles and a few dozen smaller ones.

Raids and sieges were far more common. A typical knight took part in hundreds of these.

Raids were quick, hit-and-run assaults to destroy an enemy's crops, burn his villages, and kill his **peasants**, the poor people who worked on the land. The idea was to wreck the enemy's economic base so that he could not continue fighting.

Sieges could last weeks or even months. If a town or castle was so well fortified that it could not be captured, the attacking army would surround it. This prevented anyone from going in or out, and over time the people inside would usually surrender or starve to death.

Whether a battle was large or small, short or drawn out, it was always bloody, noisy, and awash with chaotic death.

Knights typically took part in small raids and sieges. Huge battles like this one were rare.

One fourteenth-century observer vividly described a knight's emotions in battle: "Here they come! Here! There are so many—No, not as many as that—This way—that—Come this side—Press them there—News! News! They come back hurt, they have prisoners—no, they bring none back. Let us go! Let us go! Give no ground! On!"[7]

Horses and Weapons

Since the art of riding set a knight apart from a common soldier, having a good warhorse was essential. Knights rode huge horses called **chargers** that were specially chosen for their courage, strength, size, intelligence, and endurance. They were expensive and cherished—a single charger cost a fortune and a typical knight hoped to own at least two. Today's large draft horses, such as Belgians and Clydesdales, are descendants of these noble animals.

Knights used many kinds of weapons in battle. Among the most common were maces (steel and wood clubs), flails (spiked metal balls attached to chains), battle-axes, and small daggers. All of these were useful in close, hand-to-hand combat.

A knight's most important weapon, however, was his sword, which he could use both on horseback and on foot.

Protection

Of course, knights had to protect themselves as well as attack. Their earliest and simplest protection was **mail** or **chain mail**, close-fitting clothing made of tens of thousands of tiny, interlocking metal rings. Mail deflected sword blows fairly well, but it could not stop

A Knight's Armor

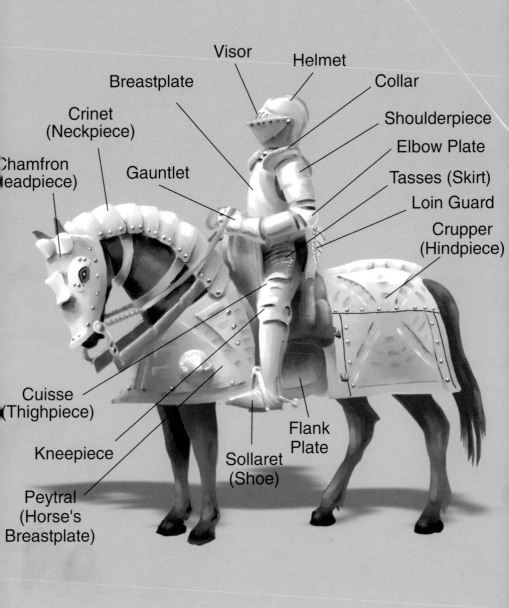

Visor

Helmet

Breastplate

Collar

Crinet
(Neckpiece)

Shoulderpiece

Elbow Plate

Chamfron
(Headpiece)

Gauntlet

Tasses (Skirt)

Loin Guard

Crupper
(Hindpiece)

Cuisse
(Thighpiece)

Kneepiece

Sollaret
(Shoe)

Flank
Plate

Peytral
(Horse's
Breastplate)

more powerful weapons such as the crossbow, which fired iron bolts. Another terrifying weapon was the halberd, a hooked spear designed to let a footsoldier snag a charging knight off his horse and then slash at him with a large ax.

To protect against such weapons, beginning in about the fourteenth century knights added iron or steel **plate**

Knights wore mail, heavy armor, and surcoats as protection from medieval weapons.

armor on top of their mail. Over this they wore heavy cloth coats called **surcoats** to keep the metal from getting too hot in sunlight.

A suit of mail probably weighed only about twenty or twenty-five pounds. However, a full suit of late-period armor—mail, plate armor, and surcoat—weighed fifty to sixty pounds, including a five- to six-pound helmet.

This is roughly as much as a modern infantryman's full pack of equipment. However, people today are generally taller and stronger than they were in medieval days, when a man's average height was around five feet two inches.

Hollywood movies depict knights in armor as slow and clumsy. A real medieval knight in battle armor could readily perform such physical feats as mounting a horse. However, if he lost his horse, an armored knight was in some danger. The weight of the armor would eventually tire him out and make him a relatively easy target.

Useful and Stylish

Early plate armor was simple, but over time skilled craftsmen refined it. They custom-made armor, often elaborately engraved and shaped, to fit individual wearers. The beauty and style of these works of art reflected the taste and status of the knights who owned them.

Armor from Spain, Germany, and northern Italy was considered especially strong and beautiful. Bertrand de Guesclin, for example, made a long trip to Spain from his native France in part to outfit himself with a suit of fine

Spanish armor. Because each suit was custom-made from hard-to-find materials, armor was very expensive. A knight could easily spend twice as much on armor as he had on one charger.

The most visible part of a suit of armor, and one of the most important, was the helmet. The earliest helmets were simple cones or flat-topped cylinders. As time went on, however, helmets became more sophisticated.

Knights were distinguished by their coats of arms. Here a brilliant yellow background bears a red antelope.

Movable visors were added that could be raised for visibility or lowered for protection. The shapes of helmets also changed greatly. A curved top, for instance, was useful because it deflected sword blows.

No matter how elaborate the helmet, however, a knight's head could never be completely protected. A knight needed to see, so—even with his visor down— the area around his eyes needed to be

This knight's coat of arms shows a green design against a white background.

Over the years, armor design became more elaborate and beautiful.

unobstructed, leaving him vulnerable. A fourteenth-century writer noted that a famous English knight, John Chandos, died of a sword thrust that drove "into the flesh under his eye . . . and entered into his brain."[8]

Identifying Each Other

An important part of a knight's battle outfit was his **coat of arms**, a unique design of shapes, colors, and pictures painted on his shield and surcoat. The legendary King Arthur's coat of arms, for instance, was a blue background with three gold crowns (later changed to thirteen to symbolize the thirteen parts of his domain).

Since knights knew each other's symbols, they could be clearly identified. This was important because helmets hid faces, and in the frenzy of battle it was otherwise difficult to tell friend from enemy.

Some knights did not live through their battles. Even if a man survived an attack, a serious wound was often fatal. Medical science was primitive then. There was no way to deaden the pain of an agonizing wound, for example, and nothing to fight infection beyond the application of herbs and a red-hot iron which would burn the wound to stop the bleeding.

Nonetheless, many knights did survive their tours of duty. Those who did headed home to relax and manage their fiefs.

CHAPTER FOUR

The Knight at Home

The arrival home from battle was a joyous occasion. The weary knight was reunited at last with his wife, children, and relatives. He became a prosperous farmer who spent much of his time in leisure pursuits.

In later centuries a wealthy knight could spend all his time at home if he wanted to. He simply avoided fighting by paying a fee to his lord.

Some knights lived in humble barracks in the castles of their lords. Others lived on lavish estates surrounded by thousands of acres of fertile farmland and rich hunting grounds. For instance, John Fastolf, a British knight of the fifteenth century, controlled vast property that included ten castles, fifteen manors, and several villages.

Most knights, however, lived on medium-sized estates of four to six hundred acres. The centerpiece of such a place was the manor house. This building, two or three stories high and made of wood and stone, was where the knight and his family lived, along with the knight's squire and other servants. Scattered farther out were farm buildings, peasant huts, a village or two, and the surrounding fields.

A Typical Morning

In addition to the knight's household, a fief needed anywhere from fifteen to thirty peasant families to maintain its crops and livestock. The knight oversaw this work.

However, it was considered beneath a knight's dignity to do any farmwork himself. A thirteenth-century writer in a book about proper knightly behavior noted that "a knight should lead a life in keeping with his status, exercising himself with hunting and enjoying those things which others provide him with [by] their labors."[9]

Some knights lived on estates near villages like this one.

A knight departs for the hunt. Knights spent many hours of the day hunting a variety of animals.

A knight's day began, as with all country people, before or at dawn when he attended church. Afterward he ate a modest breakfast, perhaps just bread washed down with wine or ale.

The rest of the morning was typically spent with farm matters. The knight consulted with his foremen and other advisers who helped him manage the estate.

A noontime dinner was the day's big meal. This usually included several courses featuring meat, bread, fruit, cheese, and occasionally, vegetables such as onions or peas.

In the Afternoon

Afternoons were usually spent in recreation. If bad weather forced them to stay inside, a knight and his family might enjoy shows by traveling jugglers or acrobats. They could also listen to musicians called **minstrels** who sang songs composed by **troubadours**, poets who wrote about the life of nobility.

Games were also popular. Knights especially liked chess because of its warlike strategy. They also loved to gamble and often bet on the games they played.

If the weather was fine a knight usually preferred to be outdoors. Hunting with bow and arrow was a favorite pastime. A knight could spend hours on horseback wielding his weapons and directing a group through woods and fields. Hunting groups typically included friends, household members, and visitors, plus a large number of dog handlers and other servants.

Knights hunted for many kinds of animals, including deer, wild boar, wolves, and birds. They always used hunting dogs, but sometimes they hunted with more exotic animals.

Falconry, the art of hunting with predatory birds, was very exciting. To train a hunting bird well, a knight had to spend many months carefully teaching it to catch other birds and return the prey to him. Because of the long time spent preparing a bird of prey to become a hunter, falconry required patience and skill. It was also extremely expensive because training and maintaining a hunting bird required endless hours of work.

Early Tournaments

The life of a wealthy gentleman farmer was too idle for some knights, who missed the excitement of battle. They eased boredom with contests called **tournaments**.

Some knights trained falcons to hunt other birds.

Tournaments were often deadly. Here, a knight collapses from his wounds.

For these mock combats groups of knights gathered to "fight" each other in teams. Winners received prizes, and captured knights were held for small, but real, ransoms.

Knights used real weapons in tournaments, and the clashes, which lasted for several days, could be savage. As a result, injuries and deaths occurred frequently; one of William Marshal's sons, for instance, was killed in a tournament.

In the beginning of the eleventh century, church authorities and the upper class strongly disapproved of tournaments. They considered them bloody, wasteful, and undignified. Henry II of England banned them completely. Eventually, however, tournaments gained popularity—even with royalty. In the last centuries of medieval times tournaments evolved into relatively non-violent, festive social occasions.

Weapons were blunted to prevent serious injury in these later contests, and less violent games replaced the fierce early battles. One of these newer games was the **joust**. Charging on horseback and wearing heavy, fancy armor, two knights tried to unseat each other with blunted lances. They tried six or eight times to knock each other off. If one lost or broke his lance, they would keep fighting with swords or other weapons. While less brutal than a full mock battle, jousts could still easily result in serious injury.

Later Tournaments

Tournaments became so popular that a knight could make a living going from contest to contest, like a modern-day rodeo cowboy. Competing in tournaments could be very profitable. In a single two-year period, for instance, William Marshal and a companion captured 103 knights in tournaments and collected handsome rewards for all.

From large viewing platforms observers cheered their tournament favorites. Noble ladies gave certain knights small tokens—such as a scarf or glove—to show that they were favorites. The knights proudly wore these tokens while competing in their ladies' names.

This idea, of a brave knight fighting in honor of a beautiful woman, represented a complex set of rules that detailed how a knight should behave. This code, which developed in the later centuries of medieval times, was called the code of **chivalry**.

Chivalry

Like tournaments, chivalry evolved as a way to make knighthood less violent and more refined than it had been in the early Middle Ages. It stressed the importance of honor, glory, loyalty, courage, and the Christian faith.

Knights sometimes fought to defend a beautiful woman's honor.

A chivalrous knight pledged to resist evil and never surrender. He also promised to display courteous and refined behavior and to hold true to the ideal of romantic love. The ideal of knightly romantic love was a love affair that was chaste—that is, the woman accepted the knight's love but refused any physical affection. Such ideals were often in sharp contrast to the reality of medieval life, which was generally harsh and brutal.

Some knights, in fact, did not live up to chivalric ideals—or even pay much attention to them. They were cruel to anyone outside their families, religion, or social level. They were unruly, uneducated, and brutal. And they did not hesitate to attack the helpless, seize valuables from the weak, or kill their enemies without mercy.

Nonetheless, many knights did strive to uphold the code. Some joined together in protective societies called chivalric orders. Among the most famous of these were the Knights Templar and the Knights of St. John. These orders formed before and during the Crusades, the long wars that sought to place the Holy Land in Christian hands.

In the centuries since medieval times, chivalry did much to create a popular image of the "knight in shining armor." This image is the one that most people today identify with knights. It continues to fascinate us, even hundreds of years after the knights themselves have disappeared into history.

Notes

Chapter 1: What Was a Knight?

1. Gutierre Díaz de Gómez, *The Unconquered Knight: A Chronicle of the Deeds of Don Pero Niño, Count of Buelna,* trans. and ed. Joan Evans. London: Routledge, 1928, p. 11.
2. Quoted in Frances Gies, *The Knight in History.* New York: Harper & Row, 1984, p. 45.

Chapter 2: Training for Knighthood

3. Quoted in Peter Speed, ed., *Those Who Fought: An Anthology of Medieval Sources.* New York: Italica Press, 1996, p. 95.
4. Quoted in A. Vesey, B. Norman, and Don Pottinger, *A History of War and Weapons, 449–1660: English Warfare from the Anglo-Saxons to Oliver Cromwell.* New York: Thomas Y. Crowell, 1996, p. 81.
5. Quoted in Joseph Gies and Frances Gies, *Life in a Medieval Castle.* New York: Harper & Row, 1974, p. 166.

Chapter 3: In Battle

6. Quoted in Stephen Turnbull, *The Book of the Medieval Knight.* New York: Crown, 1985, p. 148.
7. Quoted in Barbara Tuchman, *A Distant Mirror: The Calamitous 14th Century.* New York: Knopf, 1978, p. 63.
8. Jean Froissart, *Chronicles,* trans. John Bourchier and Lord Berners. London: Macmillan, 1895, p. 197.

Chapter 4: The Knight at Home

9. Quoted in Speed, *Those Who Fought,* p.95.

Glossary

broadsword: The most common type of sword that knights used.

charger: A warhorse, specially bred for courage, size, and strength.

chivalry: A set of rules explaining how a knight should behave.

coat of arms: The symbol a knight used to identify himself.

dubbing ceremony: The ceremony in which a man became a knight.

falconry: The sport of hunting with predatory birds. Also called hawking.

feudalism: The medieval system of providing land to knights in exchange for their services as soldiers.

fief: Pronounced "feef." A gift, usually land, given to a knight under feudalism.

joust: A contest in which two knights charged on horseback and tried to unseat each other.

lance: A wooden, steel-tipped spear, usually about twelve feet long.

mail (or chain mail): A type of armor made of thousands of interconnected iron rings.

minstrels: Wandering musicians and singers.

oath of fealty: The oath of loyalty a knight swore to his lord.

page: An apprentice, or junior assistant, to a knight.

peasant: A poor person who worked on the land belonging to a knight.

plate armor: The iron and steel armor that knights wore over chain mail.

squire: The stage of becoming a knight between page and knighthood. Squires were assistants to knights.

surcoat: A heavy cloth coat worn over armor.

tournament: A contest of warlike games held in peacetime.

troubadour: A poet who wrote about the noble life. His songs were performed by minstrels.

For Further Exploration

Christopher Gravett, *The Knight's Handbook.* New York: Dutton, 1997. This brief but informative book, with descriptions of armor and suggested activities such as making a sword and shield, was written by an authority on medieval armor.

Avery Hart and Paul Mantell, *Knights & Castles: 50 Hands-On Activities to Experience the Middle Ages.* Charlotte, VT: Williamson, 1998. Fun activities and information in this book help kids realize what life was like in medieval times.

Sarah Howarth, *The Middle Ages.* New York: Viking, 1993. This book has excellent illustrations and text about all aspects of medieval life.

Christopher Maynard, *Days of the Knights: A Tale of Castles and Battles.* New York: DK, 1998. A very entertaining and informative story about a fictional boy's adventures in the time of chivalry.

Will Osborne and Mary Pope Osborne, *Knights and Castles: Magic Tree House Research Guide #2.* New York: Random House, 2000. A companion to *The Knight at Dawn,* one of the very popular Magic Treehouse series.

Shelley Tanaka, *In the Time of Knights: The Real-Life Story of History's Greatest Knight.* Toronto, Canada: Madison Press, 2000. A nicely illustrated book about a famous knight, William Marshal.

Index

Picture Credits

On Cover: © Christie's Images/Bridgeman Art Library
© Alinari/Art Resource, NY, 28, 29
© Art Resource, NY, 9
© Giraudon/Art Resource, NY, 15, 23, 34, 36, 39
Chris Jouan, 10-11, 18, 25
© Erich Lessing/Art Resource, NY 7, 14, 22, 33
© Mary Evans Picture Library, 37
© The Pierpont Morgan Library/Art Resource, NY, 8
© Scala/Art Resource, NY, 5, 26
© Victoria & Albert Museum, London/Art Resource, NY, 30
© Visual Arts Library/Art Resource, NY, 17

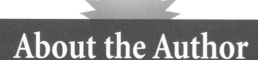

About the Author

Adam Woog is the author of many books for adults, teens, and children. His titles for Lucent Books include volumes on Harry Houdini, Elvis Presley, the Elizabethan theater, Amelia Earhart, sweatshops in the Industrial Revolution, and the Beatles. He lives with his wife and daughter in his hometown of Seattle, Washington.